Wealth Of Nations

Bangladesh

Jane Ayliffe

WAYLAND

Wealth of Nations series includes:

Bangladesh

Egypt

Ghana

Nigeria

Bangladesh is a simplified version of the title *Bangladesh* in Wayland's Economically Developing Countries series.

Cover: Foreground: villagers on their way to a festival; Inset: the front of a temple.
Title page: Bananas and other goods are brought to market by boat.
Contents page: Pumping water from a tube well.

Series editor: Paul Mason

First published in 1998 by
Wayland (Publishers) Ltd
61 Western Road, Hove
East Sussex, BN3 1JD, England

© Copyright 1998 Wayland (Publishers) Ltd

Find Wayland on the Internet at www.wayland.co.uk

British Library Cataloguing in Publication Data
Ayliffe, Jane
     Bangladesh. (The wealth of nations)
     1. Bangladesh - Economic conditions - Juvenile literature
     2. Bangladesh - Social conditions - juvenile literature
     I. Title
     954.9'2'05

ISBN 0 7502 2254 9

Typeset by Polly Goodman.
Printed and bound by Lego, Italy.

Acknowledgements
The publishers would like to thank the following for allowing their photographs to be reproduced in this book: ACTIONAID 5, 12 (bottom), 13, 16, 18, 21, 22, 28, 29, 30, 31, 32, 33, 34, 35, 36, 37, 40, 43, 45; Eye Ubiquitous 12 (top, David Cumming), 41 (Jim Holmes); Jim Holmes covers, 4, 9, 11, 15, 16, 17, 25, 26, 39, 44, 45; Panos Pictures 7 (Jim Holmes), 23 (Liba Taylor), 42 (B.Klass); Ann and Bury Peerless 1, 3, 8; Popperfoto 19, 20. Artwork by Peter Bull (6, 10, 14, 20, 24, 27, 38, 41).

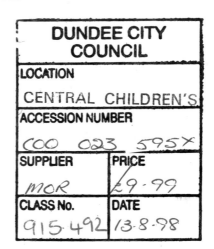

CONTENTS

INTRODUCTION

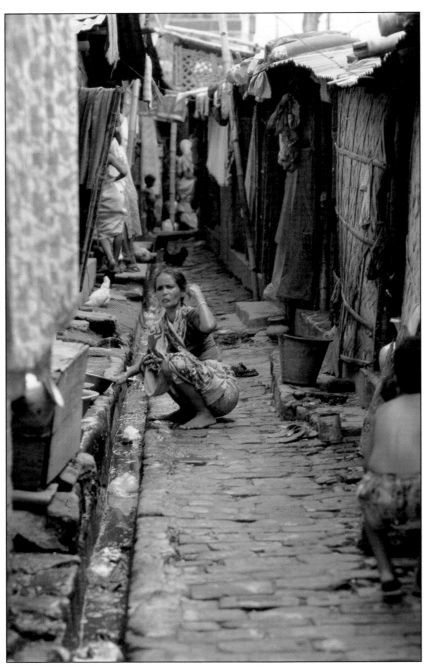

▲ A slum in the capital city, Dhaka.

Bangladesh is a country in Asia. Before 1947, it used to be part of India. The name Bangladesh means 'land of Bangla-speaking people'.

Two hundred years ago, the area that is now Bangladesh used to be very wealthy. But today, Bangladesh is the twelfth-poorest country in the world.

Many people live in slums, and cannot afford enough food. Few can afford to send their children to school.

▲ A fertile rice field being harvested.

Most people in Bangladesh are poor. But the land is very fertile and good for farming. Everyone works hard to try and improve their lives.

'My hard work, knowledge and skills keep the family going.'
– **Sobura Katum (right)**.

LAND AND CLIMATE

Bangladesh is only 147,960 square kilometres, which is less than half the size of Britain. It lies on the Tropic of Cancer.

Most of the year the landscape is lush and green. At harvest time, the rice fields turn a golden colour.

You can see ▶ the three large rivers that run through Bangladesh on this map.

6

◀ A family home by a river, which could be washed away if the river changes its path.

RIVERS

The land of Bangladesh was formed by the three huge rivers that run through it. These are the Ganges, the Jamuna and the Meghna. These rivers begin high up in the mountains north of Bangladesh, in India.

When they reach Bangladesh, the rivers form a delta. A delta is made where rivers dump sediment on to the land as they reach the sea.

Since Bangladesh is a huge delta, the land is very flat. The rivers have low banks, and every two or three years, they change their path. This can sometimes wash away people's crops and homes.

CLIMATE

Bangladesh has three seaons. From May to October is the monsoon season, when heavy rains fall.

November to February is Bangladesh's winter, when it is cooler and dryer. The dry season is from March to May, when it is hot and there is little rain.

RAINFALL IN DHAKA

	Rainfall (mm)
January	10
March	60
May	250
July	330
September	240
December	10

You can see when the monsoon rains fall in Dhaka in this chart.

Cattle trying to find grass ▶ to eat in the dry season.

FLOODS

Since Bangladesh is so flat, the rivers often flood. Most floods happen during the monsoon season, when there is heavy rain.

The monsoon floods are usually good for the land. They leave fertile sediment behind on the land.

When the floods happen at an unusual time of year, or when they are very deep, they can damage land and homes.

▲ A woman collecting water during a flood.

CYCLONES

Cyclones are huge, spinning winds that form over the sea. When cyclones form in the Bay of Bengal, huge waves are blown up Bangladesh's rivers. The waves break over the banks and damage farmland.

PEOPLE IN BANGLADESH

About 100 million people live in Bangladesh. This is nearly twice the population of Britain.

About 86 per cent of people are poor. On average, people live to be 52 years old.

LANGUAGE
Most people in Bangladesh are Bengali. They speak a language called Bangla. English is also spoken, but mainly by business people.

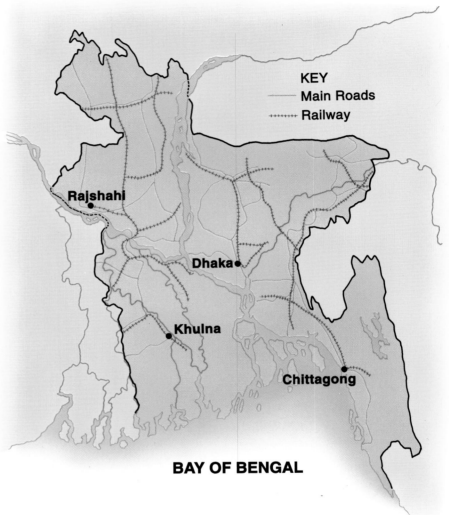

KEY
— Main Roads
+++++ Railway

BAY OF BENGAL

▲ This map shows the roads and railways in Bangladesh.

RELIGION
Most Bangladeshis are Muslims. Twelve per cent of the people are Hindu, and the rest are Christian or Buddhist.

WORK IN BANGLADESH	
Type of work	Percentage of population
Farming and fishing	72
Industry	12
Services	16

CITY LIFE

In 1992, just 16 per cent of Bangladeshis lived and worked in the cities. But each year more and more people move to the cities.

Dhaka is the capital city. Nearly 7 million people live in Dhaka, and the city is growing very fast.

▼ A busy street in Dhaka.

11

▲ A rich family travelling in a rickshaw.

RICH AND POOR

Rich people in Dhaka live in large houses and own cars. They can pay for their children to go to private school, or even to university abroad.

Many poor people in the city live in slums, in houses made from scrap wood and iron. They do not have tap water or electricity in their homes. There are more poor people in Dhaka than rich.

'I grow flowers outside our house to make it beautiful.'
— **Mohammed Firoz, aged 10 (right).**

Mohammed Firoz outside his ▶ corrugated-iron house.

▶ Amirul Haque goes to school before work. He hopes that by learning to read he can become a master technician.

WORKING CHILDREN

Many children in Bangladesh have to work to help their family. Some go to school from 7 am to 9 am, before working until 6 pm. Many other children do not get the chance to go to school at all.

WORK IN THE CITIES

Cities are important to Bangladesh because most of the wealth is produced in them.

Most work is in factories, such as steel mills and shipyards. One of the main industries in Bangladesh is making clothes. There are over 1,100 clothes factories in Bangladesh. The clothes are sold to other countries.

LIFE IN THE COUNTRYSIDE

Most people in Bangladesh live and work in the countryside. They grow crops to sell in the markets. Some crops, such as jute and tea, are also sold abroad.

Rice is the main food eaten in Bangladesh. The biggest rice crop is planted in the monsoon season, between June and July. A smaller crop is planted before the monsoon. In the dry season, winter crops such as vegetables, peppers and pulses are grown.

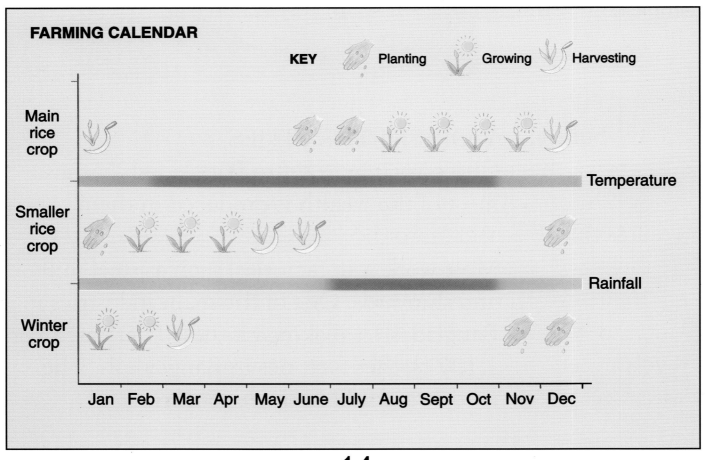

FARMING CALENDAR

KEY   Planting   Growing   Harvesting

Main rice crop

Temperature

Smaller rice crop

Rainfall

Winter crop

Jan Feb Mar Apr May June July Aug Sept Oct Nov Dec

Farm workers ▶
planting a rice
crop by hand.

WHO OWNS LAND?

Since farming is the most important activity in
Bangladesh, owning land is essential to making
a living.

Nearly all the land in Bangladesh is good for
farming, but the land is not shared out equally.
A quarter of the land is owned by 5 per cent of
the population. Over half Bangladesh's people
have less than 0.2 hectares or no land at all.

Landless people can borrow land from rich
farmers, but they have to give them over half the
harvest in return. Or the landless can work for
farmers in return for a percentage of the crops.

HOMES

People in the countryside live in a type of village, called a *bari*. These are small groups of houses, built on higher land to protect them from flooding. Poor people with no land often build their home in the *bari* of a richer family.

▲ Grain is spread out to dry in a *bari* (village).

OTHER WORK

Away from the fields, people in the countryside make things to sell, like woven rope, bags and mats. Fishing is important work, because most people cannot afford to buy meat and eat fish instead. People can also work building roads, or in service jobs such as running a shop or pulling a rickshaw taxi.

Pulling up a good ▶ fish catch in the Ganges river.

16

WHY IS BANGLADESH POOR?

WEATHER AND LANDSCAPE

Since farming is so important to most people in Bangladesh, the weather can cause sudden poverty by making a bad harvest.

◀ This sluice gate is meant to help drain flood water. But it is broken and the farmers cannot afford to repair it.

TOO MUCH WATER

Heavy flooding often destroys fields of crops and erodes land away. The high winds brought by cyclones also cause flooding near the coast, sweeping away crops, farm animals and homes.

▲ Drinking dirty water from a river.

DEFORESTATION

Deforestation is the cutting down of too many trees. This has happened in the Himalayas north-west of Bangladesh.

Deforestation increases flooding and erosion because there are no tree roots to hold the soil in place. Soil is then carried down the rivers, choking them up.

TOO LITTLE WATER

In the dry season in Bangladesh, few crops can be grown. Many people cannot earn a living in these months.

Even in the monsoon season, the rains often fail. Crops do not get enough water and there is less drinking water for people.

BRITISH RULE

When Britain took control of the region that is now Bangladesh in 1757, the British wanted to make as much money out of it as possible. So they introduced crops to be sold abroad, called cash crops. The money from the sale of these crops went back to Britain, not to Bangladesh.

Britain also changed the system of land ownership, so that some farmers were allowed to charge others rent. They banned the sale of cotton cloth from Bangladesh. So the Bangladesh cloth industry collapsed.

◀ Tying up a roll of jute. Jute is a cash crop, which was introduced by the British. It is used to make sacks and rope.

British people in Bangladesh in about 1920.

INDEPENDENCE

When India became independent in 1947, the country that is now Bangladesh was made part of a new country, Pakistan. Bangladesh was called East Pakistan, but West Pakistan was over 1,800 kilometres away.

Most of the money made from crops in East Pakistan was spent in West Pakistan. The two parts fought each other in a civil war, until Bangladesh became independent in 1971.

▼ East Pakistan (now Bangladesh) and West Pakistan between 1947–71.

DEBT

Bangladesh has borrowed a lot of money from other countries. This means it is in debt. Many people in Bangladesh are also in debt. They borrowed money from lenders after a disaster, such as a bad harvest.

It is very difficult to get out of debt, because it costs so much to pay it off. Bangladesh's debt means it has little money to spend on education or healthcare. People in debt are often forced to sell their land and belongings.

◀ A busy market in Karachi, where people can make a little money by selling their left-over crops.

▲ Children helping with the harvest.

LANDLESS FARMERS

Life is hard for people who are employed by landowning farmers. There is only work during harvest and planting time, so there often isn't enough work to go around.

Even families that once had land have lost it over the years. When parents die, their land is divided among their children, according to Muslim laws. Bangladeshis have large families, so the land is quickly divided into tiny pieces.

WOMEN

According to the Muslim laws of purdah, women should not work in public. They must cover their heads with a veil when they leave the house. Many girls do not go to school. Instead, they help their mothers or read the Qur'an, the Muslim holy book.

Many women work in private, in the homes of rich people. Others have to break the law of purdah to survive and work in the fields.

A veiled ▶ woman in public, dressed according to the Muslim law of purdah.

HOW DO YOU MEASURE POVERTY?

One way of measuring the poverty of a country is by measuring the total wealth a country produces and dividing it by the population. This measurement is called Gross National Product (GNP) per capita. 'Per capita' means 'for each person'.

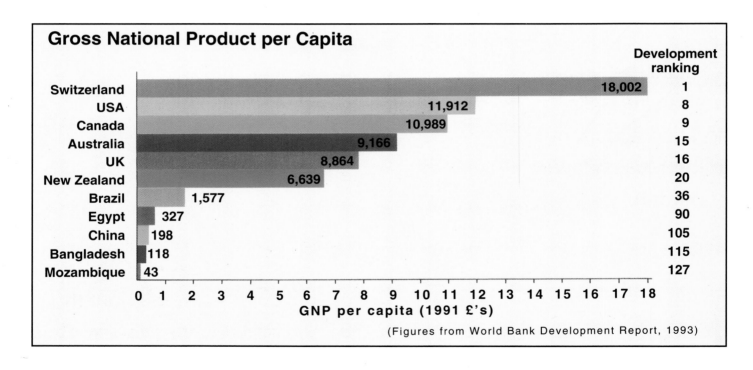

Gross National Product per Capita

Country	GNP per capita (1991 £'s)	Development ranking
Switzerland	18,002	1
USA	11,912	8
Canada	10,989	9
Australia	9,166	15
UK	8,864	16
New Zealand	6,639	20
Brazil	1,577	36
Egypt	327	90
China	198	105
Bangladesh	118	115
Mozambique	43	127

GNP per capita (1991 £'s)

(Figures from World Bank Development Report, 1993)

The graph above shows that Bangladesh has the twelfth-lowest GNP per capita. This means it is the twelfth-poorest country in the world.

24

BASIC NEEDS

Another way of measuring poverty is counting the number of people who have enough food, clean water, health care and education.

▲ Not many children in Bangladesh can afford sweets, as this girl can.

BASIC NEEDS IN BANGLADESH

Out of 110 million people in Bangladesh:
- 22 million cannot get safe drinking water.
- 21 million children do not go to school.
- Most people only live to about 52 years old.

◀ A health worker teaches women about the importance of safe drinking water.

Schools like this ▶
one are often
affected by floods.

MEASURES OF POVERTY

People are usually poor if:

- They cannot read or write.
- They have little access to clean water.
- They have little access to education.
- They have little access to farmland.
- They have little access to loans.
- They have many childhood deaths.
- They have many unplanned births.

If people do not have enough clean drinking
water, good health care and a chance for an
education, they can be thought of as poor.
In Bangladesh, a lot of people do not have
these things.

LIFE ON BHOLA ISLAND

Bhola Island is a typical region in Bangladesh. It used to be a wealthy farming region, but over the last 200 years, like the rest of the country, it has become poor.

Over half of the population are landless. Many children have never been to school and only 20 per cent of Bhola's people can read and write.

There is little clean water or health services, and in some areas, 80 per cent of children under five years old are under-nourished.

'The wealthy live in nice corrugated-iron-sheet houses. The poor live in thatched houses.'

– **Mukul Rahman, development worker.**

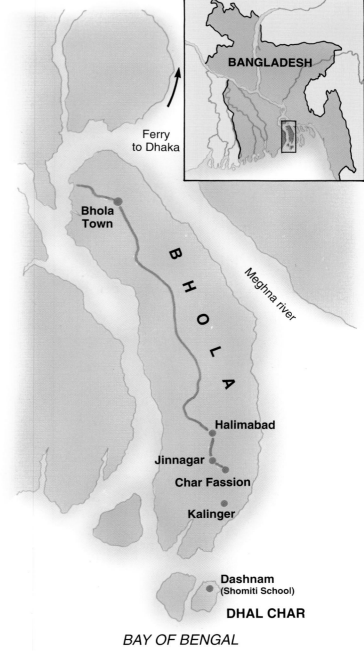

▲ This map shows Bhola Island.

Roshunara lives on Bhola Island with her husband, Mohammad Yunus, and their three children.

The family own a small plot of land. But it cannot grow much food, so Roshunara works in the fields of a farmer. She is paid in a portion of the crops she picks. One day's work picking lentils might bring her enough to feed the family for four meals.

MEALTIMES
Breakfast: Often nothing.
Lunch: Rice, possibly with some vegetables.
Evening meal: Rice, with vegetables. Sometimes fish curry.

▲ Inside the home of a poor family. The walls are made of straw.

SCHOOL

Roshunara's children do not go to school. They are like most children in Bangladesh, who help their parents farming or in other jobs instead.

Some children learn to read the Qur'an. They have their lessons at special religious schools.

▲ A boy reading the Qur'an.

FISHING

Mohammad Yunus works on fishing boats or in the rice fields. Sometimes he buys fish at the coast and carries them 8 kilometres to a large market to sell. Mohammed earns about 15 taka (15 pence) a day.

◀ Selling fish at a market.

MARKETS

There are lots of busy markets along the coast of Bhola. Most people sell crops or farm animals. But there are also stalls selling hand-made mats and rope. There are permanent shops, as well as tea stalls and restaurants.

TRANSPORT

Travelling can be difficult on the island. There is only one paved road, but most people cannot afford to take a bus. Instead, they walk, cycle or take a rickshaw. Motorbikes are just for the rich.

▲ Kebabs at a market food stall.

◄ This is the only paved road on Bhola Island. The others are dirt tracks.

FIGHTING POVERTY ON BHOLA ISLAND

People on Bhola Island are struggling to provide for their families. They want to improve their lives, but it is very difficult to escape poverty.

People need money to make money. But it costs too much to borrow money from lenders in Bangladesh.

One scheme in particular has helped people improve their lives in many different ways. It is the *shomiti* scheme.

◀ Families like this one are fighting to improve their lives.

SAVINGS SCHEME

The *shomiti* scheme is a savings scheme, which is made up of 360 clubs. The clubs are called *shomitis*. Each *shomiti* has twenty people, and meets once a week.

The *shomiti* groups help their members save money. They also lend money that can be paid back gradually at a much lower cost than borrowing from money lenders.

Some *shomiti* members use the loans to pay off debts to money lenders that are costing too much. Others buy something that will make money itself, like hoogla leaves, which can be made into mats and sold at the market.

This woman is ▶ making a mat out of hoogla leaves, to sell in the market.

▲ Women at a *shomiti* group meeting.

WOMEN AND SHOMITI GROUPS

At first, many women were worried about the *shomiti* group meetings. There would be a male charity worker there, so many of the women did not want to go to the meetings. They did not want to break the Muslim rule of purdah.

But once women who had been to a meeting told their friends about it, many more women joined a *shomiti*.

BUYING LAND

For many people, the first step in improving their lives is to own their own simple house on a small piece of land. So many people on Bhola Island have borrowed money from their *shomiti* to do this.

▼ A family outside their straw house.

'This is our house on our land. We couldn't do that without the *shomiti*.' – **Sakhina, member of a *shomiti* in the village of Jinnagar.**

INVESTMENT

A good way to pay off a loan is to invest the money into a business. It may take time, but business makes money.

Ayub Ali used a *shomiti* loan to buy tyres for the rickshaw he hired. He was able to use the rickshaw as a taxi to make money.

Finally, Ayub was able to buy the whole rickshaw, and then he paid back the loan.

Since the saving and loan scheme was set up over fifteen years ago, over £340,320 has been saved. About 96 per cent of people have paid back their loans. Over 16,000 families on Bhola Island now have access to the scheme. It means they can make their own choices and helps them take steps to improve their lives.

Ayub Ali with the rickshaw he bought using a loan.

▼ Rupoti (on the right) is learning to read. This will give her many more opportunities than her mother or grandmother, who are beside her.

SCHOOLS

Another way *shomiti* groups have given people a chance is by paying for schools. Seventy schools have been set up on Bhola Island, and the *shomiti* groups pay the teachers' wages. Now, children of even the poorest families have a chance to go to school.

Jogo Bondha Roy, the ▶ headmaster of a *shomiti* school.

36

Schools have also been set up that run in the morning and evening. This means that children can help their parents on the farm and go to school. There are also 51 schools for adults, since most people could never go to school when they were young.

The schools have increased the harvests. Children can now help their parents by reading the instructions on fertilizer packets, so the fertilizer is spread on the farmland properly.

▲ Home time is popular even at a *shomiti* school!

CLEAN WATER

To get clean water, people need wells that reach deep underground. But most people in Bangladesh cannot afford to build wells, so they have to drink dirty water from rivers which carry diseases.

Charities from abroad have been helping to build wells on Bhola Island. Over 1,000 wells have been dug so far. They have provided over 200,000 people with clean drinking water.

'Having a well here has been great for everybody! Now we have no fear of sickness.' – **Mohammed Nasim Haidan.**

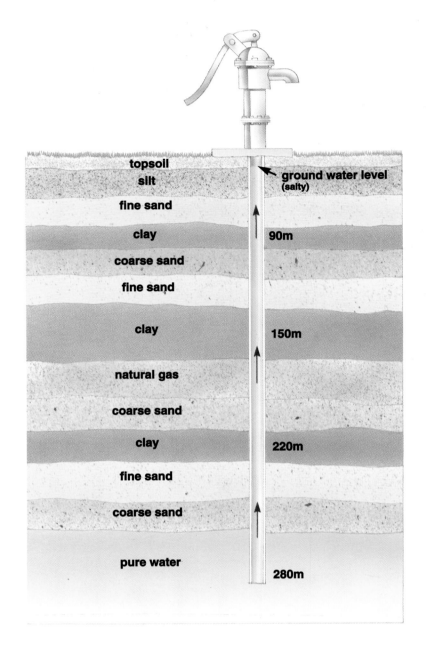

topsoil
silt
fine sand
clay — 90m
coarse sand
fine sand
clay — 150m
natural gas
coarse sand
clay — 220m
fine sand
coarse sand
pure water — 280m

ground water level (salty)

▲ This diagram shows water going up a well to the pump at the top. The safe drinking water is 250 metres below ground.

A TALE OF TWO WELLS

The best place for wells is near people's homes. That way, they don't have far to carry water. The first well in the village of Kalinger was dug too far away from most people's homes. It took the women an hour to collect water every day. So after the women protested, a second well was dug nearer their homes.

'It's us women that fetch the water, and we like our new well here!' – **Josneara.**

◄ A woman pumps water from a well.

HEALTH AND HYGIENE

Diseases such as tetanus, diptheria and polio used to affect many people on Bhola Island.

Shomiti groups have been organizing people to have injections, which immunize (protect) them from these diseases. The injections are given by the government. More and more people are learning about the importance of immunization.

Hygiene (keeping things clean) is also very important to prevent disease. Children at *shomiti* schools have been learning about hygiene, and telling their mothers what they have learnt.

Loans from *shomiti* groups are also helping families feed their children better. The number of undernourished children in some *shomiti* groups has halved in the group's first year.

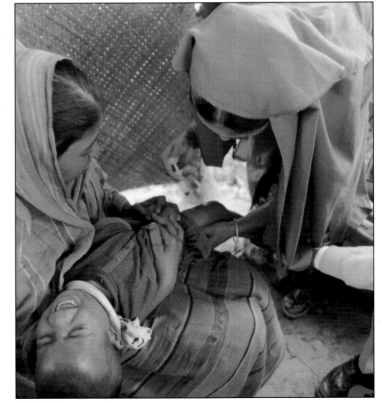

An injection is given to a child, to protect against tetanus.

▲ This woman has to make a little food go far most of the time.

▶ The chart shows how children's health has improved since the *shomiti* groups began.

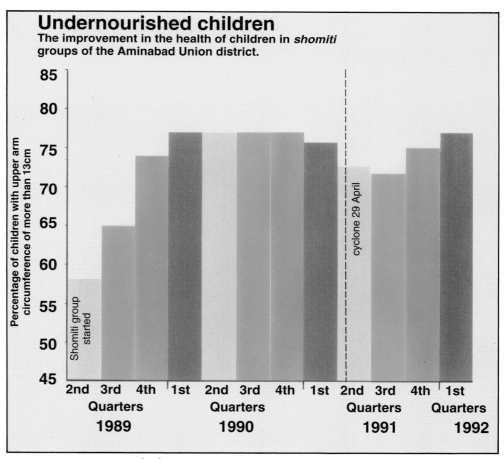

Undernourished children
The improvement in the health of children in *shomiti* groups of the Aminabad Union district.

Percentage of children with upper arm circumference of more than 13cm

85
80
75
70
65
60
55
50
45

Shomiti group started

cyclone 29 April

2nd	3rd	4th	1st	2nd	3rd	4th	1st	2nd	3rd	4th	1st
Quarters			Quarters				Quarters				Quarters
1989			1990				1991				1992

41

CYCLONE DISASTERS

Bhola Island, like the rest of Bangladesh, is at risk from cyclones. Their high winds cause flooding and can flatten buildings. In 1991, a cyclone narrowly missed Bhola Island. But crops, animals and buildings were swept away.

'When we got back to our home we found nothing. Our cattle were all dead. We searched for our home but there was nothing to recover.' – **Abdul Kader, talking about the day after the 1991 cyclone.**

▼ This town was hit by a cyclone. It flattened most of the buildings.

▲ This *shomiti* school has been built on stilts to keep it above flood waters, and its walls have been reinforced to protect it from strong winds. It can now be used as a cyclone shelter, as well as a school.

CYCLONE SHELTERS

The safest place to be in a cyclone is in a cyclone shelter. But they cost £45,000 each to build, so it will take the government a long time to provide them for everyone.

Schools built by *shomiti* groups can also be cyclone shelters if their walls are made stronger. This is much cheaper to do than building brand-new cyclone shelters.

Poverty still exists on Bhola Island, but the *shomiti* groups are helping. Loans, new schools, healthcare and protection against cyclones are helping the people improve their lives themselves, with just a little help from charities.

THE FUTURE OF BANGLADESH

Many changes are happening in Bangladesh which should help the country get richer. New rice seeds are being used, irrigation is being improved and fertilizers are helping crops.

◀ A rice shop. New types of rice should make rice crops bigger in future.

Big schemes are planned to help control river floods, and to protect against cyclones. It is important that all people in Bangladesh benefit from these schemes, not just the rich.

Other countries are also very important to the future of Bangladesh. They have been helping to run schemes such as the *shomiti* scheme on Bhola Island. They also give money towards bigger projects, such as building dams for irrigation.

A procession ▶
that is part of a
Hindu festival.
Life is not always
a struggle in
Bangladesh.

Other countries are also important for trade in the future. If they buy more food and cotton cloth from Bangladesh, it will help farmers and factory workers.

Any schemes in the future must give poor people a chance. The chapters on Bhola Island (pages 31–43) have shown how poor people are working hard to improve their lives.

◀ Poor people, like Mohammed Idris Miah, can make changes to improve their lives.

Glossary & Further information

GLOSSARY

Basic needs Things people need to survive, such as health, houses and education.

Cyclone A system of very strong winds blowing inwards in a spiral.

Delta An area of land at the mouth of a river, formed from soil sediment washed down by the river.

Gross National Product (GNP) The money a country makes within its borders, plus any money it makes from trade and overseas investment.

Hygiene Cleanliness.

Investment Putting money into a business or product so that it will make more money.

Literacy The ability to read and write.

Monsoon The wind that brings heavy rains to Bangladesh between May and October.

Purdah Islamic laws that require women to veil themselves when they go out of their homes.

Qur'an The Muslim holy book.

Rickshaw A small, three-wheeled vehicle that is powered like a bicycle.

Shomiti This word means 'club' or 'association' in Bangla. It is a group in Bangladesh that helps people to save, and lends them money that doesn't cost much to pay back.

Slums Poor, overcrowded housing.

Undernourished Without enough food.

BOOKS TO READ

Asia (Continents series), Wayland 1997.
The Ganges (River Journeys series), Wayland 1995.
Hurricanes and Typhoons and *Tidal Waves and Flooding* (A Closer Look At series), Franklin Watts.
I Am A Muslim (My Belief series) Franklin Watts.
My Muslim Life (Everyday Religions series) Riadh El Droubie, (Wayland 1997).
Traditions From India (Cultural Journeys series), Wayland 1998.

RESOURCE MATERIALS

Dhaka To Dundee examines the lives of people in Bagladesh and Britain. From Leeds Development Education Centre, 151–153 Cardigan Rd, Leeds LS6 1LJ.

Economic Issues Facing Bangladesh examines different economic issues at a variety of scales, from families to national. *People Of The Delta* examines life on Bhola Island. Both from ActionAid, 3 Church St, Frome, Somerset BA11 1PW.

Topic web and Development activities

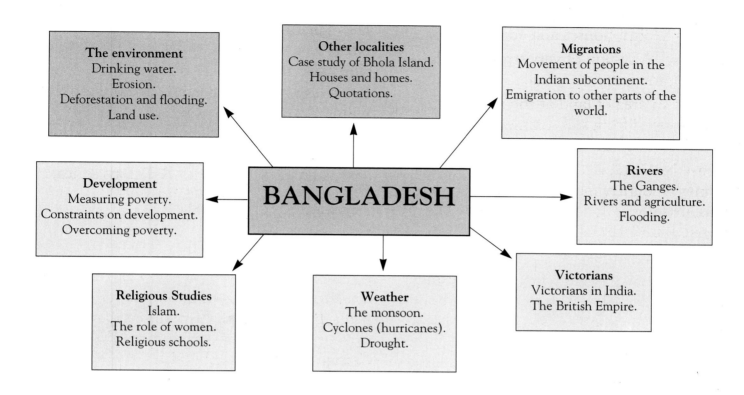

The environment
Drinking water.
Erosion.
Deforestation and flooding.
Land use.

Other localities
Case study of Bhola Island.
Houses and homes.
Quotations.

Migrations
Movement of people in the
Indian subcontinent.
Emigration to other parts of the
world.

Development
Measuring poverty.
Constraints on development.
Overcoming poverty.

BANGLADESH

Rivers
The Ganges.
Rivers and agriculture.
Flooding.

Religious Studies
Islam.
The role of women.
Religious schools.

Weather
The monsoon.
Cyclones (hurricanes).
Drought.

Victorians
Victorians in India.
The British Empire.

FURTHER ACTIVITIES

Development: Can you think of ways of testing wealth. How do the children judge how rich people are? Make a list of their responses, then ask them to look at the list on page 26. Are any of the entries the same? What are the differences between the two lists?

Weather: Use an atlas to find the rainfall figures for a city near you. Compare these with the Dhaka figures on page 8. For fun, you could make a monthly measure on the wall showing how far up the wall the water in each city would come.

Write a report on the effects of a hurricane on: a) where you live; b) Bhola Island. The Beaufort Scale tells you the effects of different windspeeds. Reports of the October 1987 hurricane in Britain might be helpful.

Other localities: Using the photos on pages 31, 33, 34, 36 and 41, make comparisons with homes where you live. You could look at building materials, cooking utensils, furnishings and bedding.

The Bhola Island chapter has information on communications, school, food and water, work, weather and religion.

Rivers: Use an atlas to find where Bangladesh's three main rivers rise. Are there things upriver that could affect Bangladesh? One example might be a dam: another would be a big city, or a steep mountain slope. How would these things affect Bangladesh?

Index

Page numbers that appear in **bold** show pictures as well as text.